Lerner SPORTS

SPORTS TEAM SMACKDOWN

US MEN'S HOCKEY VS. CANADA MEN'S HOCKEY

BATTLE FOR OLYMPIC GOLD

JASON M. BURNS

Lerner Publications ◆ Minneapolis

To all young athletes and dreamers. Practice doesn't make perfect, it makes progress. Be the best you there is, not the best that ever was.

The stats and information in this book are accurate through the 2026 Winter Olympics.

Lerner Publications Company
An imprint of Lerner Publishing Group, Inc.
241 First Avenue North
Minneapolis, MN 55401 USA

For reading levels and more information, look up this title at www.lernerbooks.com.

Main body text set in Aptifer Sans LT Pro.
Typeface provided by Linotype AG.

Library of Congress Cataloging-in-Publication Data

The Cataloging-in-Publication Data for *US Men's Hockey vs. Canada Men's Hockey: Battle for Olympic Gold* is on file at the Library of Congress.

ISBN 979-8-3480-6907-0 (lib. bdg.)
ISBN 979-8-3480-6914-8 (pbk)
ISBN 979-8-3480-6916-2 (epub)

Manufactured in the United States of America
1 – 7/15/26

TABLE OF CONTENTS

INTRODUCTION

ON THE ICE

Ice hockey is Canada's most popular sport. In the United States, the men's national hockey team has helped the sport grow with some amazing moments. The most famous Team USA win came on February 22, 1980.

The 1980 Winter Olympics took place in Lake Placid, New York. At the time, Olympic athletes had to be amateurs. That meant they were not paid to play. The US hockey team was made up of college students.

Team USA was not expected to win many Olympic games in 1980. People were surprised when they tied Sweden and then defeated Czechoslovakia, Norway, Romania, and West Germany.

Team USA players (in white jerseys) battle the Soviet Union during the 1980 Winter Olympics.

Team USA then had to face their toughest competition yet—the Soviet Union.

At the time, the Soviet Union was the most feared team in ice hockey. They had dominated the sport for many years and had beaten Team USA 10–3 just a few weeks before. But in one of the biggest upsets in the history of sports, Team USA defeated the Soviet Union 4–3. Fans and reporters called the game the Miracle on Ice.

Team Canada faced their own test against the Soviet Union in 1987. The two teams were meeting for a three-game series in the Canada Cup. The Canada Cup was the first ice hockey tournament that allowed teams with both pro and amateur athletes to compete.

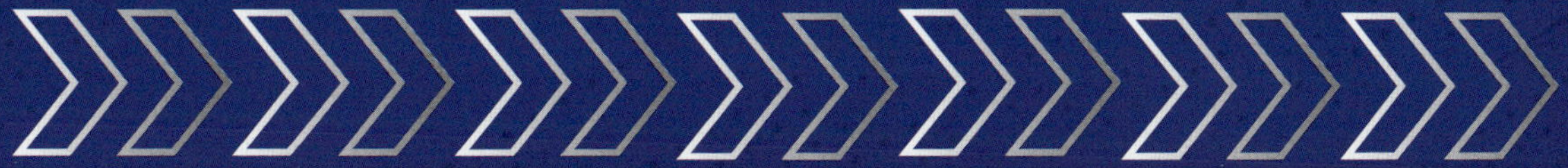

- Men's Team USA Hockey has won three Olympic gold medals.
- Team USA defeated Team Canada in the final game of the 2026 Winter Olympics in Italy.
- Canada's National Men's Team has won nine Olympic gold medals.
- Team Canada defeated Team USA in the final game of the 2010 Winter Olympics in Vancouver, Canada.

The Soviet Union won the first game 6–5. Team Canada won the second game in double overtime 6–5. The winner of the third game would take home the Canada Cup.

The Soviet Union scored quickly. Team Canada was down 3–0 in the first period. They roared back as the scoring continued. The two teams were tied 5–5 in the third period.

With little more than a minute left to play, two of hockey's all-time greats stepped up for Team Canada. Wayne Gretzky passed the puck to Mario Lemieux. Lemieux blasted the puck into the net with a wrist shot. Team Canada won the game 6–5.

The US and Canada men's hockey teams are two of the most successful national teams to ever take the ice. But which one is best? Let the smackdown begin!

Team Canada players (in red jerseys) celebrate a goal against the Soviet Union in the 1987 Canada Cup.

SMACKDOWN!

CHAPTER 1

The 1920 Summer Olympics also served as the first hockey World Championship. The United States won second place.

NEIGHBOR NATIONS

Men's Team USA Hockey was formed in 1920 to compete at the 1920 Summer Olympics in Antwerp, Belgium. The team won the silver medal that year. Team USA was originally named the United States of America Amateur Hockey Association. It changed its name to USA Hockey in 1991.

CHECK IT OUT

Pro athletes were allowed to compete in most Olympic sports starting in the 1980s. But pro hockey players did not play in the Olympics until 1998.

Canada's National Men's Team started in 1963. Before then, amateur teams played for Canada in international events. The first team that represented Canada in the Olympics was the Winnipeg Falcons. They won the first Olympic gold medal in ice hockey in 1920.

Members of Team Canada line up for a photo after beating Team USA for the gold medal at the 1924 Olympics.

Team USA Hockey and Canada's National Men's Team have a rivalry that started more than 100 years ago. Not only did the two countries meet in ice hockey's first gold medal game in 1920, but they have also faced off 20 times at the Olympics. While Team USA has dominated many other Olympic sports, ice hockey is a source of pride for Canadian players and fans. When Team Canada meets Team USA on the ice, the games are always exciting.

Members of Team USA and Team Canada shake hands after Game 6 of the 1976 Canada Cup. Team Canada defeated Czechoslovakia to win the tournament.

Team Canada celebrates their gold medal win at the 2002 Olympics.

Team Canada has won the gold medal at the Olympics nine times. Team USA has won the gold medal three times. The two teams have faced off 14 times in the World Cup of Hockey, which was formerly the Canada Cup. Team Canada has dominated Team USA in the World Cup of Hockey with a record of 10 wins, three losses, and one tie.

Canada is usually favored to win when the two teams compete against each other. Until Team USA's historic gold medal win at the 2026 Winter Olympics, the United States had gone 46 years without winning the gold medal. Team Canada has dominated the modern era of ice hockey. They won the gold medal in 2002, 2010, and 2014.

Members of Team Canada celebrate after the gold medal game at the 2010 Olympics.

Auston Matthews (top right) and other members of Team USA cheer together after winning gold at the 2026 Olympics.

Both teams are filled with some of the greatest players in the National Hockey League (NHL). Playing with and against each other in the NHL only strengthens the rivalry. Veterans such as Connor McDavid and Nathan MacKinnon will continue to anchor Team Canada, while young talent such as Seth Jarvis and Macklin Celebrini represent the next generation. Team USA's talent pool continues to develop as well. And current superstars such as Auston Matthews and Jack Hughes are young enough to represent the United States again at the 2030 Winter Olympics in France.

CHAPTER 2

Team USA defeated the Soviet Union 3–2 during the 1960 Winter Olympics.

AMAZING MOMENTS

The Team USA Hockey men won their first Olympic gold medal on February 28, 1960. They were trailing 4–3 against Czechoslovakia after the first two periods. In the third period, Team USA was unstoppable with six goals. They won the game 9–4. Team USA was undefeated throughout the tournament, including a 2–1 win over Team Canada.

The Miracle on Ice in 1980 captured the attention of sports fans in the United States. But to win the gold medal, Team USA still had to face off against Finland after defeating the Soviet Union. The US players were exhausted, and a few were injured, but they refused to give up. Team USA defeated Finland 4–2 to win the gold medal.

The rivalry between Team USA and Team Canada received international attention on February 22, 2026. The two countries were meeting in the final game of the 2026 Winter Olympics. It was a tough game for both teams. They were

Team USA and Team Canada have faced each other 20 times in the Winter Olympics.

Team USA rising star Jack Hughes scored four goals in the 2026 Olympics, including the game-winner that earned gold for the United States.

tied 1–1 at the end of regulation time. Jack Hughes scored a dramatic game-winning goal in overtime for Team USA. They defeated Team Canada 2–1 to win the gold medal.

Canada has celebrated a lot of amazing moments in ice hockey. Many fans believe the country's best was on September 28, 1972. Team Canada was facing the Soviet Union in an eight-game hockey event called the Summit Series. With only 34 seconds left in the final game, Paul Henderson scored a goal to lead Team Canada to a 6–5 victory. Had the game ended in a tie, the Soviet Union would have won the tournament.

CHECK IT OUT

Sidney Crosby was the youngest player in NHL history to reach 100 points in a season. He was also the youngest player to win a scoring title in a major North American sports league. He was only 18 at the time. Fans and sports writers nicknamed him Sid the Kid.

Team Canada went 50 years without winning an Olympic gold medal. They defeated Team USA at the 2002 Winter Olympics in Salt Lake City, Utah, to win the country's first

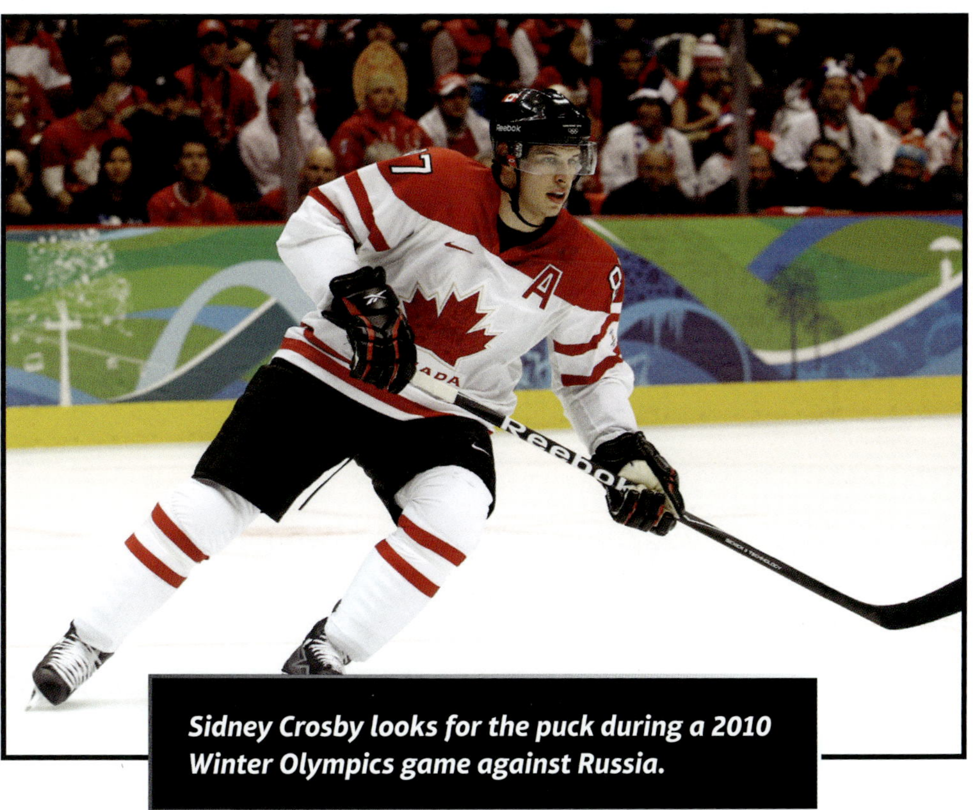

Sidney Crosby looks for the puck during a 2010 Winter Olympics game against Russia.

Joe Sakic helped Team Canada win gold at the 2002 Olympics.

gold medal since 1952. Joe Sakic scored two goals and had two assists in the game. The final score was 5–2. Team Canada dominated the sport for the next two decades.

Team USA faced Team Canada again in the final game of the 2010 Winter Olympics in Vancouver, Canada. Unfortunately for Team USA, Sidney Crosby played for Team

Canada. Crosby is one of the biggest stars in the NHL. He scored the now famous "golden goal" in overtime to break a 2–2 tie and win his country another gold medal. It was the best-attended gold medal game in Olympic history with 17,748 fans in the arena.

In 1980, Ken Morrow became the first player to win an Olympic gold medal and a Stanley Cup championship in the same year.

CHECK IT OUT

Of the 20 players on the 1980 Team USA Hockey roster, 13 went on to play in the NHL. Defenseman Ken Morrow spent his whole pro career with the New York Islanders and won four Stanley Cup titles in a row.

CHAPTER 3

Jim Craig guards the net after making a save during the 1980 Olympics. Craig played three seasons in the NHL.

TOP PLAYERS

Jim Craig was the goalie for Team USA during the 1980 Winter Olympics. He played every minute of the tournament. Craig made 36 saves in the Miracle on Ice game, helping Team USA defeat the Soviet Union 4–3. He played for three teams in the NHL from 1980 to 1984.

Some hockey fans consider Patrick Kane to be the best US-born player of all time. He is the all-time points leader among US-born players in the NHL. He won three Stanley Cups with the Chicago Blackhawks and is one of only 50 players in the NHL to score 500 goals in his career. He helped Team USA win the silver medal at the 2010 Winter Olympics.

Patrick Kane skates toward the goal during the 2016 World Cup of Hockey.

Although he was injured during the gold medal match, Jack Hughes kept playing and led Team USA to victory.

Jack Hughes was the hero for Team USA at the 2026 Winter Olympics. He scored the game-winning goal in overtime to lead the United States to its first gold medal since 1980. Hughes was the first overall pick in the 2019 NHL Draft. He has played his entire NHL career for the New Jersey Devils, where he has set multiple records.

Most hockey fans say Team Canada star Wayne Gretzky is the greatest player in NHL history. He holds over 50 NHL records, including most goals in a single season, with 92. He won four Stanley Cups with the Edmonton Oilers and was the

NHL Most Valuable Player nine times. He joined the Hockey Hall of Fame as soon as he retired in 1999. He helped Team Canada win the Canada Cup in 1987.

Mario Lemieux is another Hall of Fame player who had a big impact on Team Canada. He was captain of the team in 2002 and helped Team Canada win its first Olympic gold medal in 50 years. Lemieux was the first overall pick in the 1984 NHL Draft. He played 17 seasons in the league, all for the Pittsburgh Penguins. He won the Stanley Cup two times as a player and three times as an owner of the Penguins.

Nicknamed the Great One, Wayne Gretzky is the only NHL player ever to score more than 200 points in a single season.

Many fans consider Sidney Crosby one of the best hockey players of all time. He is a member of the Triple Gold Club. That means he has won the Stanley Cup, the Olympic gold medal, and the World Championship gold medal. Crosby was the first overall pick in the 2005 NHL Draft. He scored the "golden goal" in overtime at the 2010 Winter Olympics, leading Team Canada to victory over Team USA.

Sidney Crosby has led Team Canada to two Olympic gold medals, one World Championship gold medal, and one World Cup of Hockey gold medal.

CHAPTER 4

Jack (left) and Quinn Hughes (right) were one of two sets of brothers on the 2026 Team USA Olympic team. Brady and Matthew Tkachuk were also part of the team.

CHOOSE YOUR CHAMPION

The US and Canada men's national teams are both legendary, but which one comes out on top? There's no right or wrong answer. Different people will have different opinions.

Team USA has won three Olympic gold medals. Their wins have all been dramatic and have brought many new fans to the sport. The Miracle on Ice game captured the attention of the entire country. And hockey fans will never forget Jack Hughes's overtime goal at the 2026 Olympics.

Team Canada has won nine Olympic gold medals. They are always one of the best teams on the ice at the Olympics and other big events. Their historic wins in the Canada Cup and the Summit Series are considered some of the best games ever played in the sport. And some of the biggest legends in ice hockey have played for Team Canada.

Team Canada celebrates their gold medal at the 2014 Olympics.

The rivalry between Team USA and Team Canada is known for intense games, close scores, and last-minute goals.

Both teams have done a great job representing their countries in the sport, but Team Canada has more medals and a better record than Team USA. Canada also has a better record in head-to-head matchups. For that reason, Team Canada wins this skating smackdown.

What do you think? Did we get it right? Think about why or why not and make your own choice!

SMACKDOWN TIMELINE

MEN'S TEAM USA HOCKEY

1920 Men's Team USA Hockey begins as the United States of America Amateur Hockey Association. The team appears in its first Olympic Games, winning a silver medal.

1924 The first Winter Olympics is held. Team USA wins a silver medal.

1933 The team wins its first gold medal at the World Championships.

1960 Team USA wins its first Olympic gold medal.

1980 Team USA defeats the Soviet Union in an upset that fans call the Miracle on Ice. The US team goes on to win a gold medal by defeating Finland.

1996 Team USA wins the first-ever World Cup of Hockey, defeating Team Canada in the final game.

2002 Team USA loses to Team Canada in the finals of the 2002 Winter Olympics in Salt Lake City, Utah.

2026 Jack Hughes leads Team USA to its first Olympic gold medal since 1980.

CANADA'S NATIONAL MEN'S TEAM

1920 The Winnipeg Falcons win the first-ever Olympic hockey gold medal for Canada.

1963 Team Canada is founded by David Bauer.

1972 The team defeats the Soviet Union in the Summit Series.

1987 Wayne Gretzky and Mario Lemieux lead Team Canada to victory in the Canada Cup.

2002 Team Canada wins its first Olympic gold medal in 50 years.

2010 A new era of dominance begins as Sidney Crosby helps lead Team Canada win another Olympic gold medal.

2014 Team Canada is undefeated throughout the Olympics, winning another gold medal.

2023 At the World Championships, the team wins its fourth gold medal in eight years.

2026 Team Canada falls to Team USA in the Olympic gold medal game.

GLOSSARY

assist: a pass that leads directly to a goal by a teammate

draft: when teams take turns choosing new players

overtime: an extra period played to determine a winner when the score is tied

period: one of three 20-minute sections of a hockey game

point: a goal or an assist in a hockey game

regulation time: the standard length of a game, not including overtime

rivalry: when two teams compete against each other over a long period of time

Soviet Union: a former country in eastern Europe and northern Asia that existed from 1922 to 1991

Stanley Cup: the NHL's championship trophy

tournament: a series of games played to determine a champion

wrist shot: a quick shot made by snapping the blade of the stick quickly forward

LEARN MORE

Anderson, Josh. *G.O.A.T. Hockey Centers.* Lerner Publications, 2024.

Burns, Jason M. *US Women's Hockey vs. Canada Women's Hockey: Battle for Olympic Gold.* Lerner Publications, 2027.

Jack Hughes: Meet the Athlete
https://www.nbcolympics.com/news/jack-hughes-meet-athlete

Kiddle: Mario Lemieux Facts for Kids
https://kids.kiddle.co/Mario_Lemieux

Team USA Hockey: Men's Teams and Events
https://teamusa.usahockey.com/mensteams

Walker, Tracy Sue. *Wayne Gretzky: The Great One*. Lerner Publications, 2023.

INDEX

PHOTO ACKNOWLEDGMENTS

Image credits: Focus on Sport/Getty Images, p. 4; B Bennett/Getty Images, p. 6; Elsa/Getty Images, p. 7; Elsa/Getty Images, p. 7; Library of Congress/Getty Images, p. 8; Topical Press Agency/Getty Images, p. 9; Denis Brodeur/Getty Images, p. 10; Jamie Squire/Getty Images, p. 11; Alex Livesey/Getty Images, p. 12; Gregory Shamus/Getty Images, p. 13; B Bennett/Getty Images, p. 14; Houston Chronicle/Hearst Newspapers via Getty Images/Getty Images, p. 15; Elsa/Getty Images, p. 16; Bruce Bennett/Getty Images, p. 17; ADRIAN DENNIS/Getty Images, p. 18; Focus on Sport/Getty Images, p. 19; Focus on Sport/Getty Images, p. 20; Tom Szczerbowski/Getty Images, p 21; Elsa/Getty Images, p. 22; Bruce Bennett/Getty Images, p. 23; Martin Rose/Getty Images, p. 24; Elsa/Getty Images, p. 25; Bruce Bennett/Getty Images, p. 26; Steve Powell/Getty Images, p. 27.

Cover: Cal Sport Media via AP Images; AP Photo/Carolyn Kaster.